arts & architecture

JANUARY

ANNOUNCING THE "CASE STUDY" HOUSE PROGRAM

ANNOUNCEMENT

the case study house program

Because most opinion, both profound and light-headed, in terms of post war housing is nothing but speculation in the form of talk and reams of paper, it occurs to us that it might be a good idea to get down to cases and at least make a beginning in the gathering of that mass of material that must eventually result in what we know as "house—post war".

Agreeing that the whole matter is surrounded by conditions over which few of us have any control, certainly we can develop a point of view and do some organized thinking which might come to a practical end. It is with that in mind that we now announce the project we have called THE "CASE STUDY" HOUSE PROGRAM.

The magazine has undertaken to supply an answer insofar as it is possible to correlate the facts and point them in the direction of an end result. We are, within the limits of uncontrollable factors, proposing to begin immediately the study, planning, actual design and construction of eight houses, each to fulfil the specifications of a special living problem in the Southern California area. Eight nationally known architects, chosen not only for their obvious talents, but for their ability to evaluate realistically housing in terms of need, have been commissioned to take a plot of God's green earth and create "good" living conditions for eight American families. They will be free to choose or reject, on a merit basis, the products of national manufacturers offering either old or new materials considered best for the purpose by each architect in his attempt to create contemporary dwelling units. We are quite aware that the meaning of "contemporary" changes by the minute and it is conceivable that each architect might wish to change his idea or a part of his idea when time for actual building arrives. In that case he will, within reason, be permitted to do so. (Incidentally, the eight men have been chosen for, among other things, reasonableness, which they have consistently maintained at a very high level.)

Elizabeth A.T. Smith

CASE STUDY HOUSES

1945 – 1966

The California Impetus

TASCHEN

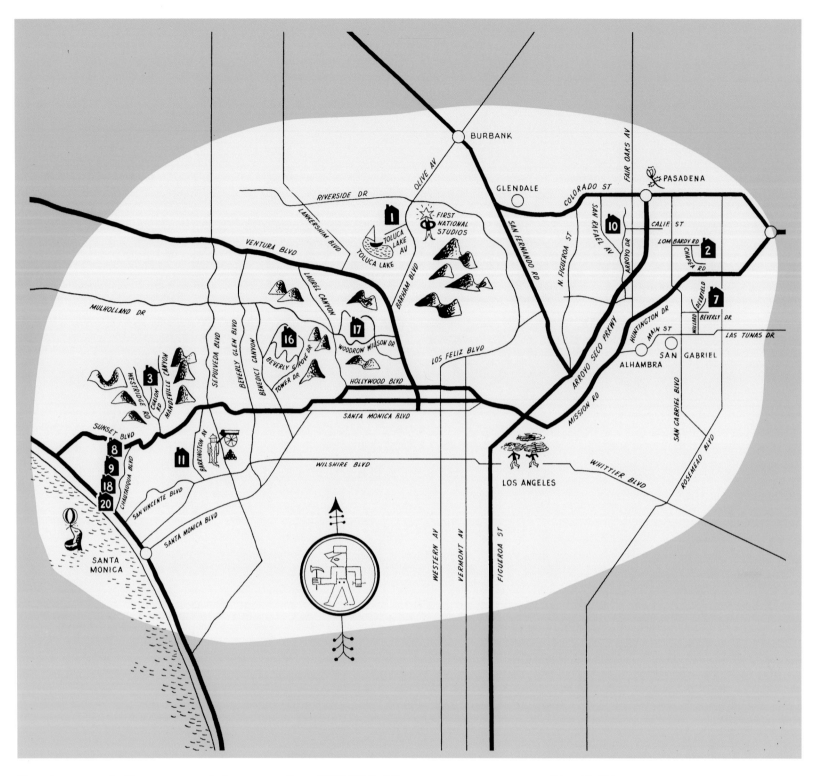

Illustration page 1 and 2: The announcement of the Case Study House program in *Arts & Architecture*, January 1945, edited by John Entenza
Illustration page 4: Map of greater Los Angeles with location of the Case Study Houses

©2013 TASCHEN GmbH
Hohenzollernring 53, D-50672 Köln
www.taschen.com

Original edition: © 2007 TASCHEN GmbH
Editor: Peter Gössel, Bremen
Project management: Swantje Schmidt, Bremen
Design and layout: Gössel und Partner, Bremen;
Sense/Net Art Direction, Andy Disl and Birgit
Eichwede, Cologne, www.sense-net.net
Cover design: Sense/Net Art Direction, Andy Disl and
Birgit Eichwede, Cologne, www.sense-net.net
Text edited by: Susanne Klinkhamels, Cologne,
Avinus, Berlin
Principal photography: Julius Shulman
Notes on the Furnishings by: Shannon and
Peter Loughrey

Printed in China
ISBN 978-3-8365-1301-2

To stay informed about upcoming TASCHEN titles,
please request our magazine at
www.taschen.com/magazine, find our app for iPad
on iTunes, or write to TASCHEN America,
6671 Sunset Boulevard, Los Angeles, CA 90028, USA;
contact-us@taschen.com; Fax: +1-323-463-4442.
We will be happy to send you a free copy of our
magazine, which is filled with information about all
of our books.

Contents

Introduction

The Case Study House program, initiated by *Arts & Architecture* magazine in 1945 in Los Angeles, remains one of America's most significant contributions to architecture at mid-century. Conceived as low-cost, experimental modern prototypes, the thirty-six designs of the program epitomized the aspirations of a generation of modern architects active during the buoyant years of America's post-World War II building boom.

The motivating force behind the Case Study House program was John Entenza, a champion of modernism and editor of the avant-garde monthly magazine *Arts & Architecture*. Entenza envisioned the Case Study effort as a way to offer the public and the building industry models for low-cost housing in the modern idiom, foreseeing the coming building boom as inevitable in the wake of drastic housing shortages during the depression and war years. Using the magazine as a vehicle, Entenza's goal was to enable architects to design and build low-cost modern houses for actual clients, using donated materials from industry and manufacturers, and to extensively publish and publicize their efforts. Prior to the program's official beginning in 1945, Entenza had already sponsored competitions in the magazine for small house design for the coming postwar period, anticipating architects' growing interest in the subject and providing an outlet for their ideas.

Architects who participated in the program did so at the invitation of Entenza himself, and therefore the roster of participants clearly reflects his personal predilections rather than a comprehensive overview of American, or even Californian, approaches to low-cost modern house design. During the initial years, an improvisatorial spirit dictated many of Entenza's choices of architects and designs. Several early projects conceived as Case Studies were never built, e.g. Richard Neutra's "Alpha House", because they lacked actual sites or clients. Neutra later realized the slightly adapted "Alpha House" plan for other clients; this house, however, was not published in *Arts & Architecture* and did not form an official part of the Case Study House program. Those that were built often changed greatly from the architects' original vision, owing to building material shortages or other difficulties surrounding the undertaking of construction in the immediate postwar years. A few of the early built houses were even brought into the program after being designed in order to continue some degree of momentum for the Case Study effort during breaks in its continuity. In one instance, Entenza himself served as the client for a Case Study house designed by Charles Eames and Eero Saarinen, while Charles and Ray Eames themselves were the clients for their own Case Study House.

The first Case Study House presented in the February 1945 issue of the magazine was a design by Julius Ralph Davidson, characterized by simple, industrial materials, a compact plan, and an informal disposition. While the published design was not built, a second, redesigned version for a different site was constructed the following year. It was not until the late 1940s, but especially during the 1950s, that the Case Study architects were able to fully embrace the ideal of experimentation with industrial materials and construction systems that underlay the thinking behind the program's genesis. Stemming from the successes achieved in the early part of the program and, most importantly, from the increased economic prosperity and technological advances of this period, a number of additional significant Case Study Houses were realized on sites in Los Angeles and in other cities of the region, such as Long Beach, Thousand Oaks, and La Jolla, for affluent clients enthusiastic about modern architecture and design. During this later period, few of the designs remained unbuilt, and the program even began to venture into tract housing and apartment design.

The best known Case Studies are the steel and glass houses by Charles and Ray Eames, Craig Ellwood, Pierre Koenig, and Raphael Soriano. From among the program's diverse examples, these approximate most closely the spirit of International Style modernism in their rigorous application of industrial construction methods and materials to residential architecture. The program also encompassed a sizable body of work that is less overtly technological but no less modern. These are post-and-beam, wood-framed houses by such architects as Thornton Abell, Julius Ralph Davidson, Richard Neutra, Rodney Walker, and the firms of Buff, Straub & Hensman and Killingsworth, Brady & Smith. Although less crisp and austere than the steel-framed Case Studies, these too employed modular, standardized parts, and were equally conceived as prototypes for mass production.

Nevertheless, despite the renown and notoriety of the Case Study House program, it must be remembered that its houses represent but one episode in the history of postwar Los Angeles modernism. Numerous highly regarded architects active during the same period, such as R. M. Schindler, Harwell Harris, Gregory Ain, Gordon Drake, Carl Maston, and John Lautner, among others, did not contribute designs to the program, since the roster of participants was determined personally by John Entenza. Consequently, many of these architects' residential designs did not benefit from the same degree of publicity or recognition that association with the Case Study House program provided in its day through publication in *Arts & Architecture* and in other national and international journals, as well as in Esther McCoy's pioneering 1962 book *Case Study Houses: 1945–1962*. Recent scholarship has contributed to a more balanced historical record of the rich diversity of mid-century modernism in southern California, of which the Case Study House program remains emblematic.

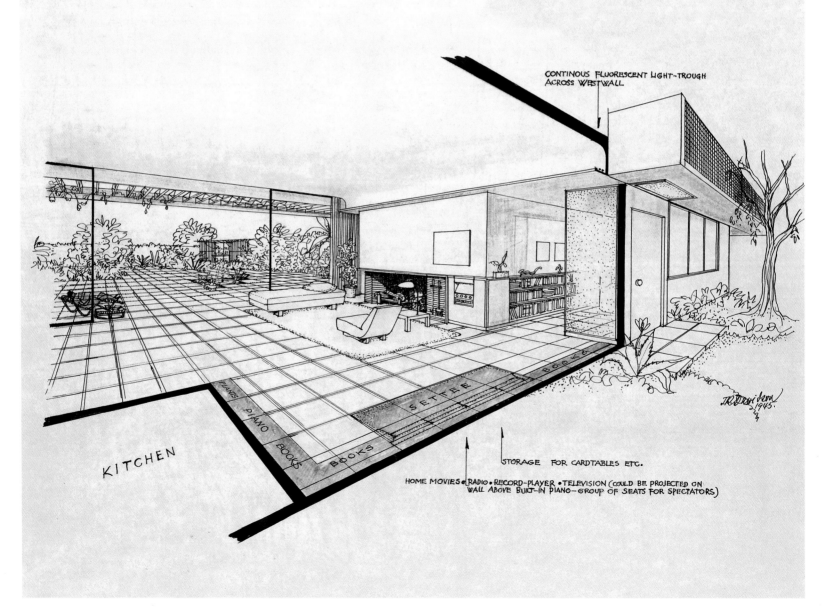

CONTINOUS FLUORESCENT LIGHT-TROUGH
ACROSS WESTWALL

KITCHEN

STORAGE FOR CARDTABLES ETC.

HOME MOVIES • RADIO • RECORD-PLAYER • TELEVISION (COULD BE PROJECTED ON
WALL ABOVE BUILT-IN PIANO-GROUP OF SEATS FOR SPECTATORS)

1945–1948 ▸ **CSH#1**

Toluca Lake Avenue, North Hollywood
Julius Ralph Davidson

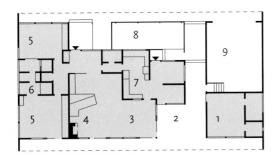

Ground plan
1 Guest, 2 Outdoor eating, 3 Dining, 4 Living,
5 Bedroom, 6 Bath, 7 Kitchen, 8 Service yard,
9 Garage

Opposite page, top:
Elevation

Opposite page, bottom:
Sectional perspective of living room

The first design for the Case Study House program, published in February 1945, was not actually the first to be built. When realized in 1948 on a different site, the house had undergone some significant changes. Davidson conceived the first version of the design for hypothetical clients as a two-story structure built of simple, industrial materials. It was planned for a maximum of spatial efficiency, with extensive built-in components and flexibility in terms of future growth and usage of the house and property. As clients for this design did not materialize, Davidson revised his concept to suit the needs of a family who came forward in 1948 with a site in North Hollywood. The result was a compact, efficiently planned one-story house of standard wood frame construction on a concrete slab, within which such materials as aluminum siding, plywood, asphalt tile flooring and Formica work surfaces were utilized.

Below left:
Rear terrace

Below right:
Dining room
Hanging lamp by George Nelson, manufactured by
Howard Miller, c. 1952, spun plastic fiber over steel wire

1945–1947 ▶ CSH#2

Chapea Road, Chapman Woods/Arcadia
Sumner Spaulding and John Rex

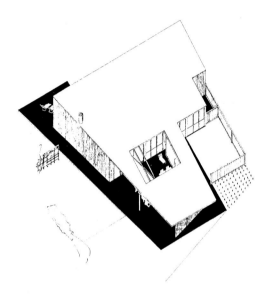

Aerial perspective

Like its predecessor in the Case Study House program, this design underwent profound changes from initial conception in 1945 to built reality in 1947. Its first version was designed by architect Sumner Spaulding, whose goal was to provide an expansive, well-organized space oriented to relaxed family living and entertaining as well as ease of household management. When built in the suburb of Arcadia on an acre of flat land amid orange trees, the house had been redesigned by Spaulding with a partner, John Rex. Straightforward and simple, it was wood-framed with extensive areas of glass; the interior incorporated black asphalt flooring, admired by the architects for its color and texture. A distinctive undulating brick wall situated alongside the motor court and connecting to the house's entrance provided an additional noteworthy feature to this design.

Opposite page, top:
Rear exterior

Opposite page, bottom left:
Front entrance from motor court

Opposite page, bottom right:
Side view of rear

Right:
Ground plan
1 Reception, 2 Living, 3 Dining , 4 Kitchen,
5 Laundry, 6 Service yard, 7 Storage,
8 Garden storage, 9 Car shelter, 10 Heat,
11 Master bedroom, 12 Bathroom, 13 Child's room,
14 Children's yard, 15 Dining terrace,
16 Living terrace, 17 Motor court

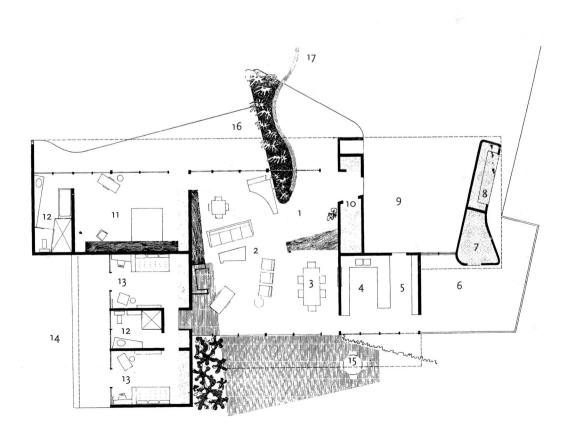

1945–1949 ▶ CSH#3

Chalon Road, Los Angeles
William W. Wurster and Theodore Bernardi

Opposite page:
Living room
Upholstered living room furniture and side table by
Hendrik van Keppel and Taylor Green, manufactured
by Van Keppel-Green. Coffee table by Isamu Noguchi,
manufactured by Herman Miller, c. 1947. Birch wood
supports, glass top. Desk (background) by George
Nelson, manufactured by Herman Miller, c. 1947.
Birch-veneered plywood, leather top and steel frame

Exterior perspective by Arne Kartwold, 1945

Originally envisioned to be sited adjacent to the first design for Case Study House #1, this house was
later built in the Mandeville Canyon area of Los Angeles. It underwent few changes from initial
concept to built reality. Focusing on issues of space, flexibility, and low cost, the house contained no
formal living room in its H-shaped plan. Instead, the architects designated a "living garden" that
incorporated an actual enclosed garden within an open living area as the center of the family's social
life. Responding to their ideal of an informal lifestyle between indoors and outdoors, their design
provided additional related features that reflected this interest, such as a carport instead of an
enclosed garage and a workroom alongside the kitchen. Wurster and Bernardi, unlike some of their
contemporaries, omitted extensive built-in components in order to allow greater freedom to the
occupants in furnishing and utilizing the space. They did, however, specify a color scheme that was
based on the hues of native planting surrounding the site.

**Rear exterior with outdoor furniture
by Van Keppel-Green**

Right:
Roof plan

Opposite page, above:
Living Room
Settee by Jens Risom, c. 1946, manufactured by
H. G. Knoll. Lounges and table by Hendrik van Keppel
and Taylor Green, manufactured by Van Keppel-Green.
Lamp by Kurt Verson, manufactured by Kurt Verson

Opposite page, below left:
Living Room
Coffee table by Isamu Noguchi, manufactured by
Herman Miller. Dining set by Hendrik van Keppel and
Taylor Green, manufactured by Van Keppel-Green.
Buffet by George Nelson, manufactured by Howard
Miller, c. 1947. Walnut veneer

Opposite page, below right:
Exterior, side view

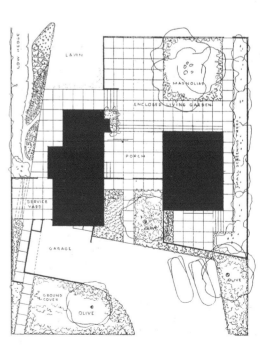

1945 ▶ CSH#4, Greenbelt House

unbuilt
Ralph Rapson

Opposite page:
Aerial perspective facing north-east

Below right:
Perspective sketch of court elevation

This innovative design was among the most unconventional of the entire Case Study House program, and remained unbuilt. Rapson, one of only two architects who contributed to the program from outside California, imagined a house encompassing nature in a significant way directly within its plan. He called his design a "greenbelt house" to indicate what he felt was a radical transformation of standard patterns of family living, and in an extensive group of preparatory drawings he explored numerous alternatives to conventional plans and structural systems. The final design was an open, pavilion-like structure bisected completely by an interior greenbelt of planting that separated the communal spaces of the house from the bedrooms. Rapson specified a modular panel construction system within either wood or steel framing as well as various industrial building materials and radiant floor heating, and his drawings indicate identifiable modern furnishings as well as such topical and futuristic touches as a Jeep in the carport and a commuter helicopter hovering overhead.

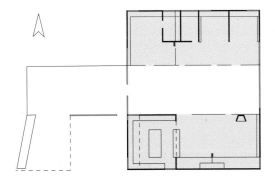

Site plan

1945 ▶ CSH#5, Loggia House

unbuilt
Whitney R. Smith

This unrealized design took the form of four rooms within a garden—a radical rethinking of the conventional house plan. Eliminating unnecessary spaces and features such as an entrance hall or breakfast nook, Smith instead emphasized the primacy of outdoor living. Extensive flexibility was provided in the way the rooms could either be opened up to form larger, flowing spaces or be separated from each other by means of sliding partitions. Smith specified adobe brick within a steel frame for the house's construction system, with accents of glass block on the façade, and brick and cork flooring throughout. Smith's unusual plan and unconventional choice of materials led to his design being designated the most extreme as well as the most "native Californian" of all the Case Study houses, and it was never carried beyond the preliminary design phase.

Top:
Scale model

Above:
Perspective looking east

Right:
Ground plan
1 Living room, 2 Loggia, 3 Dining, 4 Kitchen,
5 Bedroom, 6 Lavatory, 7 Bath, 8 Master
bedroom, 9 Guest bath, 10 Guest room,
11 Heater, 12 Carport

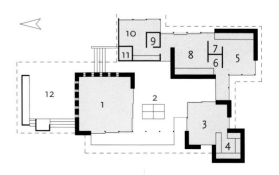

1945 ▶ **CSH#6, "Omega"**

unbuilt
Richard Neutra

The first of several designs for Case Study Houses by Neutra, this and another unbuilt companion house (Case Study House #13, "Alpha") were conceived for fictional families residing on adjacent lots. The houses were therefore designed in relation to one another and, while not identical, shared common features in terms of materials and general disposition. The Omega house was cruciform in plan, permitting the incorporation of four outdoor courtyards, each with a distinct function (entrance court, social court, sports court, and practical service court). It presented a roof profile characteristic of Neutra in its gentle slope and wide overhang, and was to have been built predominantly of redwood and glass in a vocabulary typical of that employed by the architect in this later phase of his career.

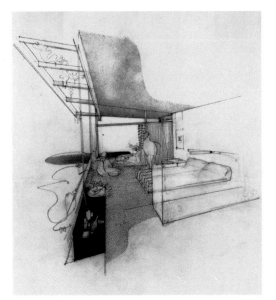

Top:
Perspective of exterior

Center:
Scale model

Left:
Perspective sketch of master bedroom

Right:
Ground plan
Notes C1 to C4 designate the four "courtyards" for entrance, living area, leisure and services, structuring the exterior along the same lines as the interior.

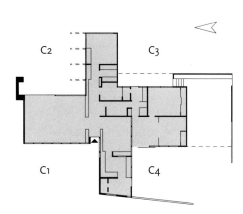

1945–1948 ▶ CSH#7

North Deerfield, San Gabriel
Thornton Abell

Opposite page, above:
Perspective of rear and outdoor living area

Opposite page, below:
Bedroom
Chair by Hendrik van Keppel and Taylor Green,
manufactured by Van Keppel-Green

Below right:
Rear and outdoor living area
Furniture by Van Keppel-Green

The first version of this house was significantly different from that which was built in 1948 in San Gabriel. The clients were an employee of a company that provided roofing materials for many of the Case Study Houses and his family. Responding to their specific needs and preferences, Abell situated a centralized activity zone for the family between the living room and kitchen, allowing for separation of spaces as well as the possibility of combining them into one larger, open area when needed. The principle of zoning for different functions also extended into the outdoor spaces in the orientation of its terraces and patios. The primary material used by Abell in the house's construction was lightweight concrete block, along with plywood and other accents such as the Pioneer-Flintkote roof provided by the company at which the client was employed.

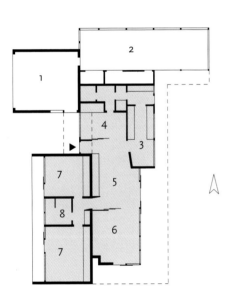

Ground plan
1 Garage, 2 Lath house, 3 Kitchen, 4 Study or Guest,
5 Activity, 6 Living, 7 Sleeping, 8 Bath

1945–1949 ▶ CSH#8, Eames House

Chautauqua Boulevard, Pacific Palisades
Charles and Ray Eames

Opposite page:
Living Room
Lounge chair #670 and #671 by Charles and Ray Eames, manufactured by Herman Miller. Coffee table by Charles and Ray Eames, custom made for this house. Seating area by Charles and Ray Eames, custom made for this house. Couch (foreground) by Charles and Ray Eames, manufactured by Herman Miller

Right:
Exterior

Initially designed jointly by Charles Eames and Eero Saarinen, the house was substantially modified during the construction process by Eames and his wife Ray, an artist and designer, to maximize its spatial area. The final design consists of two adjacent double-height pavilions—one used as a residence and one as a studio/workshop space. Demonstrating the possibilities of technologically based construction methods and materials, it is built entirely of industrial, prefabricated components including steel, glass, asbestos, and Cemesto board according to a modular system. The building's rectilinear character and structural assertiveness are enlivened by the use of a variety of textures, colors, and materials orchestrated by Ray Eames. Although conceived to be prototypical, it is a highly personal reflection of the seamless coexistence of work and leisure characteristic of these prominent American designers' unique way of life.

Above left:
Living room interior
Sculpture by Alexander Calder and chair by
Eero Saarinen

Above right:
Studio
Side chair by Charles and Ray Eames, manufactured by
Herman Miller. Dining table (far left) "DTW" by
Charles and Ray Eames, manufactured by Herman
Miller. Coffee table by Charles and Ray Eames,
manufactured by Herman Miller

Below:
Ground plan

Right:
Layout in *Arts & Architecture*, December 1945

Opposite page:
Studio with stairs leading to upper level

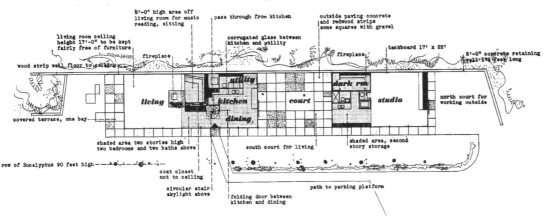

1945–1949 ▶ CSH#9, Entenza House

Chautauqua Boulevard, Pacific Palisades
Charles Eames and Eero Saarinen

Opposite page:
Living room with view to bedroom

Right:
Rear and outdoor living area
Furniture by Van Keppel-Green

Perspective showing structural framing system

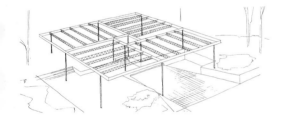

Sited adjacent to the Eames House, this house for John Entenza shared certain similarities but for the most part presented a completely different set of concerns. Indeed, the houses were considered to be "technological twins but architectural opposites" by a writer in a contemporary journal shortly after their completion. Changed very little when built from how it had been originally published in 1945, the design of the house combined a rigorous steel and glass construction system with an interior in which structure was concealed within plastered and wood-paneled surfaces. One of the first steel-framed Case Study Houses, the design of this simple cubic plan allowed for great flexibility. Entenza required very little private space, preferring instead extensive space for entertaining; the built-in seating and conversation area within this open, flowing space facilitated this activity.

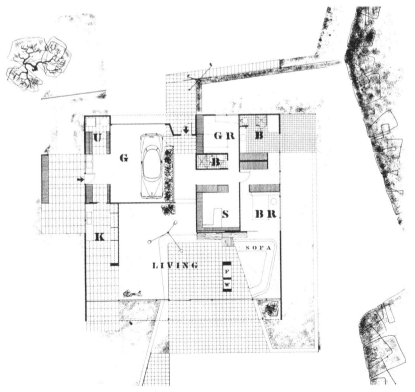

Living Room
Coffee table "ETR" by Charles and Ray Eames,
c. 1951, manufactured by Herman Miller. Plastic
laminated plywood, steel wire bases. Chairs "DCM",
"LCW", "LAR" by Charles and Ray Eames. Bench
by George Nelson, manufactured by Herman Miller

Left:
Ground plan
All functions, including the garage, are organized
within a square plan. Kitchen (K), utility room (U),
guest room (GR), bath (B), study (S) and bedroom
(BR) are situated around the living room.

Opposite page:
Terrace with view of Case Study House #8
Outdoor furniture by Hendrik van Keppel and
Taylor Green

1945–1947 ▶ CSH#10

San Rafael Avenue, Pasadena
Kemper Nomland and Kemper Nomland, Jr.

Opposite page:
Rear exterior

Right:
Living Room
Upholstered chairs by Hendrik van Keppel
and Taylor Green. Settee by Jens Risom, c. 1946,
manufactured by H. G. Knoll

Ground plan
1 Entrance, 2 Gallery, 3 Guest room, 4 Studio,
5 Dressing room, 6 Bath, 7 Bed and sitting,
8 Living area, 9 Dining area, 10 Breakfast bar,
11 Kitchen, 12 Laundry, 13 Garage

The house, the residence of a father and son team of architects, was added to the Case Study program after its completion in 1947 since many of the original designs had not been realized. Although not conceived originally within it, the house exemplified the goals of the program as a simple, low-cost modern building. Its primary construction system was wood, post and beam framing with large walls of glass, set over a concrete slab. Located on a sloping site, it was divided into three levels—studio and garage flanking the entrance, a middle zone of bedrooms, and on the lowest level, the kitchen and living area. A sloping roof with broad overhangs covered the entire house, paralleling the ground and providing a relationship to the site that was lacking in many of the other Case Study designs. Further integration with the landscape was provided by the possibility of opening up the interior dining space completely to the outdoors by means of a large sliding glass partition.

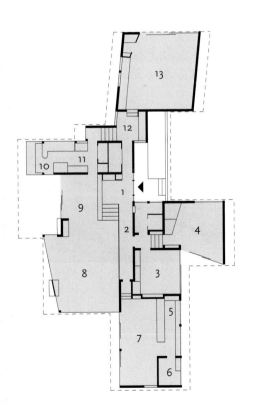

1945–1946 ▶ CSH#11

South Barrington Avenue, Los Angeles
Julius Ralph Davidson

Entrance

Opposite page:
Rear and outdoor living area
Furniture by Van Keppel-Green

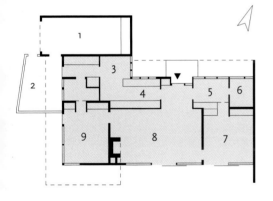

Site plan
1 Garage, 2 Service yard, 3 Eating, 4 Cooking,
5 Dressing, 6 Bath, 7 Sleeping, 8 Living,
9 Study/Guest/Child

Right:
Living Room
End table by Hendrik van Keppel and Taylor Green,
manufactured by Van Keppel-Green

This house became the first of the Case Study designs to be constructed on a site in West Los Angeles. Its clients were the advertising manager for *Arts & Architecture* magazine and his family. Despite the small size (1,100 square feet) and simplicity of the project, the architect and contractors faced many difficulties and delays in realizing the house because of material shortages still in effect after World War II. To some extent, they felt their ideas about using more experimental building methods and materials such as steel and aluminum had been compromised. Nonetheless, this first built Case Study succeeded as a compact, economical design, the efficient plan of which was especially noteworthy. Wood-framed with glass walls on a concrete slab with asphalt tile flooring, it presented a modest façade to the street, marked as "modern" by its flat roof. Following its completion, the house was toured by 55,000 visitors as part of the Case Study House program's advertising effort, launching the program's public presence.

1946 ▸ CSH#12

unbuilt
Whitney R. Smith

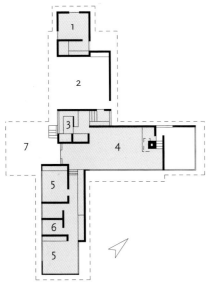

This second Case Study design by Whitney R. Smith reflected the architect's ongoing commitment to fundamentally rethinking the plan of the house according to the special needs of its proposed inhabitants. Describing in *Arts & Architecture* his ideas about the development of special interests and hobbies as one of the hallmarks of postwar living, he oriented the design for this project around the avocation of his hypothetical clients as horticulturalists. The X-shaped plan of the house enabled its interiors to be situated in close proximity to extensive garden areas defined by open lath walls and roofs. Although different in configuration, this design was not dissimilar to Smith's earlier Case Study project in terms of aspiration to achieve an integration of sheltered and open spaces.

Ground plan
1 Guest room, 2 Carport, 3 Kitchen, 4 Living room,
5 Bedroom, 6 Bathroom, 7 Lath house

Scale model

1946 ▶ **CSH#13, "Alpha"**

unbuilt
Richard Neutra

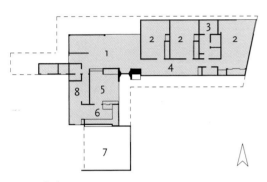

Ground plan
1 Living room, 2 Bedroom, 3 Bathroom, 4 Family
activities, 5 Dining room, 6 Kitchen, 7 Garage,
8 Laundry

Intended as a companion project adjacent to Neutra's Case Study House #6, "Omega", this house extended the vocabulary employed in that design but configured the plan differently. His hypothetical clients—relations of the family in the adjacent house—were a couple with three children, and Neutra amply provided for their social and leisure activities with the presence of a large outdoor patio and a detached lath house specifically devoted to the children of both families. He employed strategies such as paving to link the two houses and their social spaces and envisioned the interior as being able to open up extensively to the outdoors by means of sliding glass walls. Other innovative features were ideas about using interior spaces for dual functions as needed, and the provision of many thoughtful details including a toilet for each bedroom and specific spaces for various household appliances and tools.

Perspective sketch of rear exterior

1947 ▶ CSH#15

Lasheart Drive, La Canada
Julius Ralph Davidson

Opposite page:
Living room with view to outdoor terrace

Rear and outdoor living area
Furniture by Van Keppel-Green

Nearly identical in plan and appearance to Davidson's earlier Case Study House #11, this home was constructed in the La Canada region of Los Angeles, originally envisioned as the first in a tract of several contiguous Case Study Houses on adjacent lots. Built of plaster and fir siding over wood framing, it was compact in size at 1,300 square feet and characterized by extremely efficient interior planning, one of Davidson's hallmarks. Like its predecessor, Case Study #11, the house was designed with walls of sliding glass at the rear, opening to an outdoor patio that expanded the available living space for its inhabitants. While the goal of building contiguous houses as part of the Case Study program was not achieved here, this house—constructed by contractors from Davidson's plans as a speculative venture—was the only one in the program to truly embody its goal of replicability.

1946–1947 ▶ **CSH#16**

Beverly Grove Drive, Beverly Hills
Rodney Walker

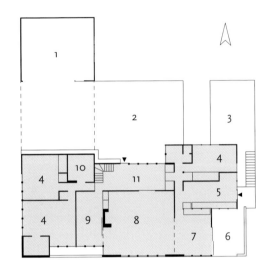

Ground plan
1 Garage, 2 Paved patio, 3 Service yard,
4 Bedroom, 5 Kitchen, 6 Outdoor dining,
7 Dining, 8 Living, 9 Study, 10 Bathroom,
11 Loggia

This design for the architect's own house was another unanticipated inclusion in the Case Study program, and the third house to be built under its aegis. Aspects of the house reflect the influence of R. M. Schindler, for whom Walker had once worked, in its multi-leveled silhouette that in part responded to the sloping landscape of its hillside site. At 2,000 square feet, it was the most spacious of the Case Studies, and incorporated features that differentiated it from others in the program, such as the inclusion of a large, skylit entrance hall, a sitting room in the main bedroom, and the provision of space for servants' quarters. Yet despite these relatively formal features, the house's simple, modular wood construction system, organization of the plan into clearly defined, yet flexible, public and private zones, and ample indoor/outdoor spaces were elements common to those of the other Case Study house designs.

Opposite page:
Aerial view

Right:
Living Room
Lounge chair by Alvar Aalto, manufactured by Finmar LTD. Couch and circular coffee table manufactured by Thonet Industries

1947 ▶ CSH#17

Woodrow Wilson Drive, Los Angeles
Rodney Walker

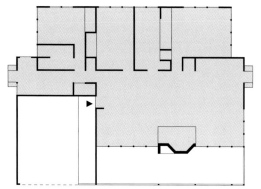

Ground plan

This reductive design situated at the base of a hillside consists of a rectangular plan in which the public rooms occupy the front of the house while the private spaces of bedrooms and baths are positioned at the rear. Built atop a flat pad of elevated earth, it was approached by a curving driveway and entered via either a covered walkway or an open carport. It was designed to include a terrace opening off the living and dining room, accessed by means of sliding glass walls and shaded by an expansive roof overhang. In 2001 the building was stripped down to the frame for reconstruction.

Perspective of exterior

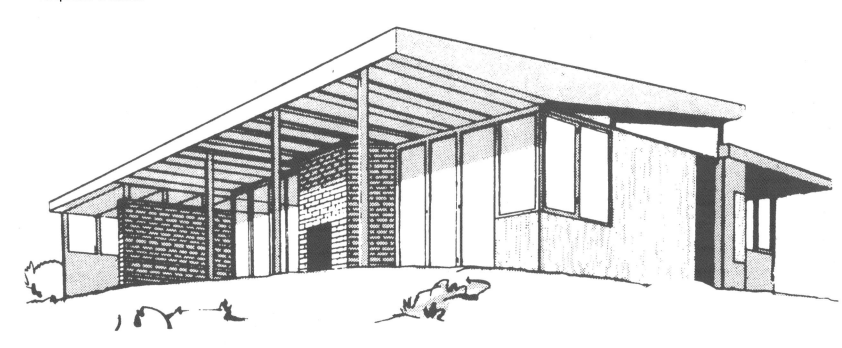

1947–1948 ▸ CSH#18, West House

Chautauqua Boulevard, Pacific Palisades
Rodney Walker

Sited on land near what would soon become a colony of Case Study Houses in the Pacific Palisades area of Los Angeles, Walker's house #18 was more highly finished in plan and details that his earlier #17. He employed a construction system similar to that of his own house, #16—positioning wood framing at 3-foot intervals to achieve strength and symmetry in the structure, as well as economy and efficiency in the building process. Because of the drama of the site and its ocean view, the major public rooms in the U-shaped plan of the house were all oriented to take advantage of it, and were provided with glass walls. The most unique and noteworthy interior feature is a large, floor-to-ceiling brick fireplace, faced with copper, that dominates the living room, and around which the roof is raised to accommodate clerestory windows.

Above:
Rear and outdoor living area
Furniture by Van Keppel-Green

Right:
Living room
Settee by Jens Risom and lamp by Greta
Magnusson Grossman

Ground plan
1 Entry, 2 Dining/Living, 3 Kitchen, 4 Bedroom,
5 Bath, 6 Service yard, 7 Garage, 8 Garden room,
9 Pool

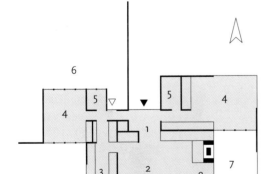

1947–1948 ▶ CSH#20, Bailey House

Chautauqua Boulevard, Pacific Palisades
Richard Neutra

Opposite page:
Exterior from the west

Below:
Exterior from the south

Richard Neutra was the most established and best-known of the architects to participate in the Case Study House program. His design for the Bailey House was characteristic of the direction of his work in the late 1940s. Simple and elegant despite its extremely small size, the house was constructed of glass, steel, and wood in a rectangular plan with a low-slung profile. Presenting a modest face to the street, the house opened up at the rear to a garden beyond with large sliding glass walls, affording its public rooms as well as its bedrooms a direct visual and spatial connection to the outdoors. Its clients were a young family who had specified the need for a compact, economical house but anticipated the possibility of growth and increased resources; indeed, they commissioned Neutra to design additions to the house three times over subsequent years. Providing for increased bedrooms as well as living spaces, these additions seem organic to the house's original design, as Neutra himself had considered the possibilities of future expansion from the beginning.

Living Room
Armchair by Alvar Aalto, manufactured by Finmar LTD,
c. 1931/32 (this example c.1947). Bench by George
Nelson, manufactured by Herman Miller, c. 1947

Right:
Site plan

Living Room
Lamp (far left) by Greta Magnusson Grossman, manufactured by Ralph O. Smith. Armchairs by Alvar Aalto, manufactured by Finmar LTD, c. 1931/32 (this example c.1947)

Left:
Side view of bedrooms opening onto outdoor spaces

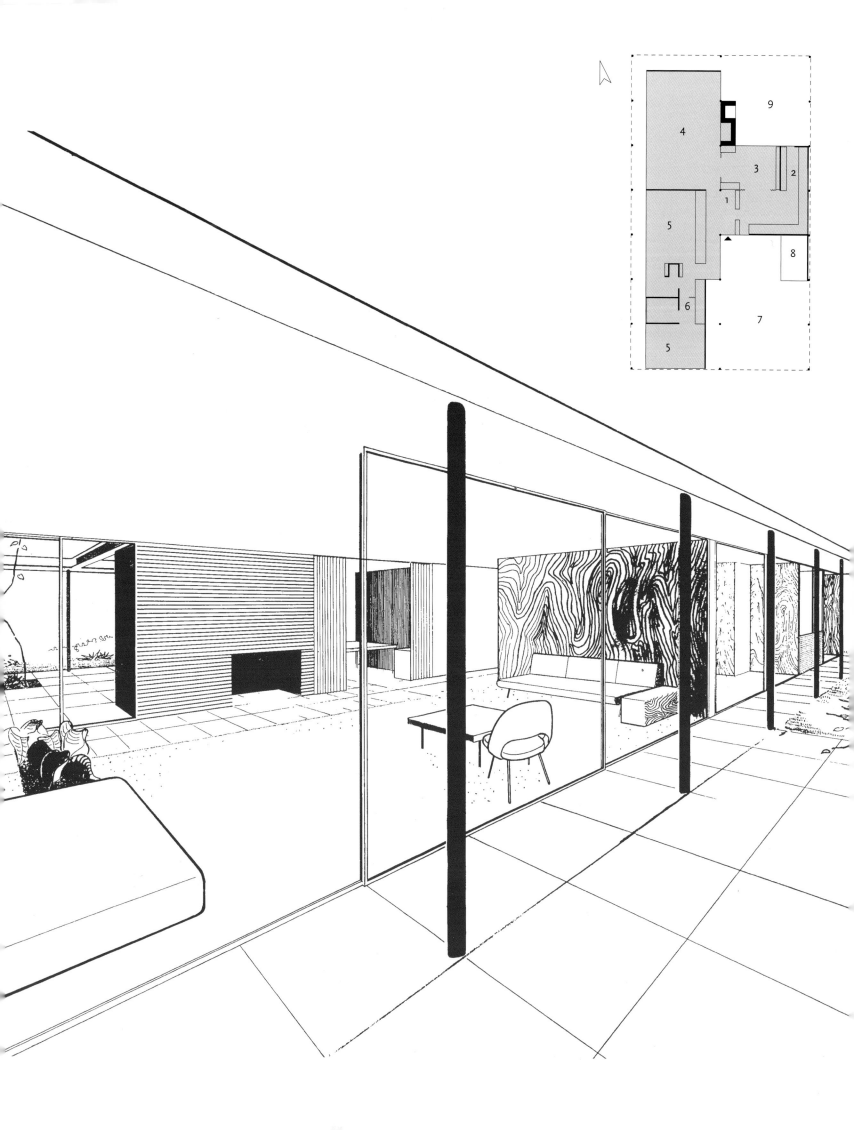

1950 ▶ **CSH 1950**

Ravoli Drive, Pacific Palisades
Raphael Soriano

Opposite page:
Perspective of living room

Opposite page, top:
Ground plan
1 Foyer, 2 Kitchen, 3 Dining room, 4 Living room,
5 Bedroom, 6 Bath, 7 Carport, 8 Storage, 9 Semi-
enclosed patio

Below:
Rear exterior and terrace

This rigorously executed Case Study manifests architect Raphael Soriano's commitment to technology in his use of steel framing for its structure. In its interiors, however, he utilized a variety of materials, such as brick, stucco, wood paneling, and carpeting—perhaps as a concession to more traditional tastes and in recognition of the fact that steel, glass, and concrete would be less palatable to the public at this moment of high visibility for the Case Study House program. Approached from the street, the house presents an extremely minimal, closed form, but it opens up in the rear to a view made possible by the wide structural framework of the 10 by 20 foot modular steel framing elements. In addition, it incorporates an outdoor terrace that appears to emerge from the living spaces within by the extension of the steel roof around its perimeter and the shared wall of brick with the adjacent living room.

1952 – 1953 ▶ **CSH#16**

Bel Air Road, Bel Air
Craig Ellwood

Opposite page:
**Rear exterior with views of living room
and terrace**

Entrance and carport

Ellwood's pavilion-like design for Case Study House #16 was the first of three houses he contributed to the program. Trained as an engineer, Ellwood had a keen interest in the application of industrial materials and techniques to architecture. The primary materials of the house were steel, glass, and concrete, yet they were used with an extreme elegance and sensitivity. Walls in this house approximate freestanding units in both the interior and parts of the exterior, where translucent glass panels screen the house from the street. Inside, Ellwood departed from the use of conventional floor-to-ceiling walls, instead configuring walls as floating panels inset into the exposed steel frame. The design manifests a high degree of rationality throughout, yet also a sensuality in terms of its finishes, textures, and details. The exterior patio, too, was well defined for relaxed, outdoor living and entertaining, including among its features a large stone chimney complete with fireplace and electric barbecue spit.

Living room

Right:
Bedroom and adjacent courtyard

Kitchen and eating area

Right:
Site plan

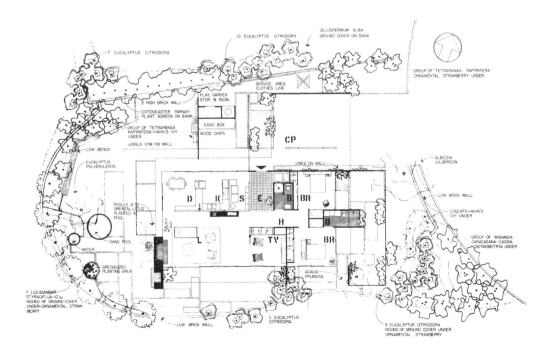

1954–1955 ▶ CSH#17

Hidden Valley Road, Beverly Hills
Craig Ellwood

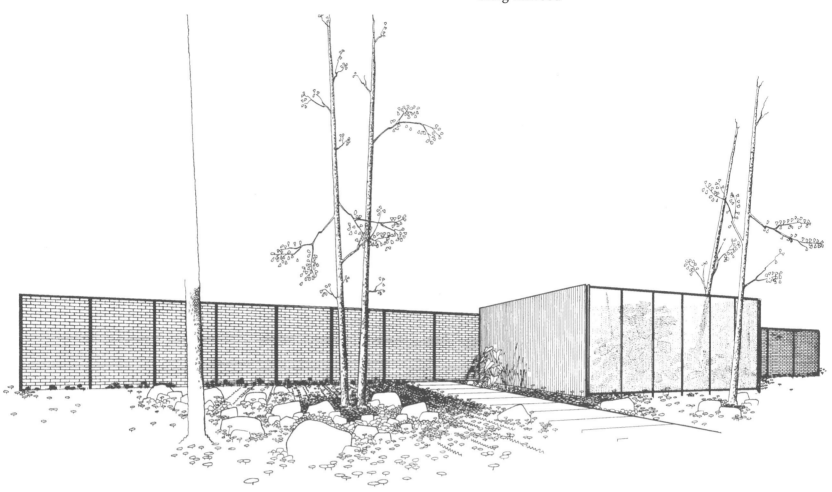

Above:
Perspective of entrance

Right:
Rear exterior with terrace and pool

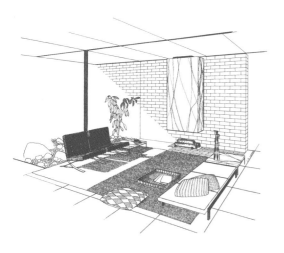

Nearly twice the size of any of the previous Case Study Houses, this design was built for a family with four children. A far more luxurious house not only in terms of its size but also in terms of its amenities, it incorporated such features as a swimming pool, tennis court, maid's quarters with bath, screened patio space for each child's bedroom, a spacious bath and dressing area off the master bedroom, and extensive provision for appliances including televisions, hi-fi, and film projection. U-shaped in plan, this spacious house grouped the bedrooms along one wing, perpendicular to the dining room, kitchen, and living room, all of which accessed the pool terrace through sliding glass doors. Like Ellwood's earlier Case Study, this one was characterized by an exposed steel frame, walls of glass, and the use of infill panel material such as translucent glass and brick. Only a few years later, however, it was altered by subsequent owners in a pseudo-neoclassical style that rendered the design unrecognizable as a Case Study House.

Above:
Perspective of living room by Jerrold Lomax

Right:
Rear exterior at night

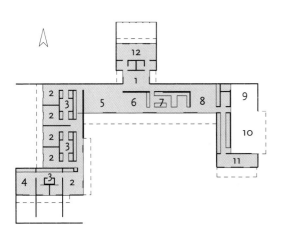

Ground plan
1 Entry, 2 Bedroom, 3 Bath, 4 Study, 5 Living,
6 Dining, 7 Kitchen, 8 Recreation room, 9 Service yard,
10 Carport, 11 Hobby shop, 12 Maids

1956–1958 ▸ **CSH#18, Fields House**

Miradero Road, Beverly Hills
Craig Ellwood

Opposite page:
Terrace
Lounge chair and ottoman by Hendrik van Keppel and Taylor Green, manufactured by Van Keppel-Green, c. 1939, produced from 1946 until 1966. Painted tubular steel with cotton yacht cord. Table by Hendrik van Keppel and Taylor Green, manufactured by Van Keppel-Green, c. 1951. Painted tubular steel and glass

Living room with view to dining room and terrace

Using a prefabricated steel frame and wall panel system, Case Study #18 was Ellwood's most successful attempt at integrating industry into the design and construction of a house. The result was an elegant, yet somewhat sturdier and more elaborate, design than that of Ellwood's previous Case Studies, in which he painted the steel frame blue and incorporated finish materials such as terrazzo flooring, wood paneling, and a mosaic design by the client on the building's exterior facing the pool. Simple and rectangular in plan, it positioned one large and two small bedrooms on one side of a living room and music room at the house's center, opposite the kitchen, breakfast area, courtyard, dining area, and entrance. Features of the house included numerous electrical outlets and the most up-to-date appliances, including a built-in system for vacuum cleaning. Like its predecessor in the program, #17, this house was also transformed beyond recognition by later owners.

Entrance and carport

Right:
Living room
Bench by George Nelson, manufactured by Herman Miller, c. 1955. Upholstered solid wood modular frames and laminated table on steel base. Chairs "Coconut" by George Nelson, manufactured by Herman Miller, c. 1956. Vinyl or fabric upholstery over foam rubber on metal frame with steel wire base.

Opposite page, above:
Rear exterior with terrace and pool

Opposite page, below:
Rear exterior
Drawing by Jerrold Lomax

1957 ▶ CSH#19

unbuilt
Don Knorr

This unbuilt design was the first Case Study to be located outside southern California. Its site was an acre of wooded land near San Francisco, and it was designed for a young family with one child. Organized as an H-shaped plan, it was composed of two wings connected by a glazed hallway—one containing a child's sleeping and play area with guest quarters, and the other the living and dining room, kitchen, master bedroom, and study. This somewhat unusual organization was underscored by another unconventional feature—the placement of the pool and barbecue at a distance from the house instead of being more integrated with it as a design for indoor/outdoor living. Furthermore, function and convenience were deemphasized in the design in favor of formal and even sculptural features, both in the interior and in the landscaping surrounding the house.

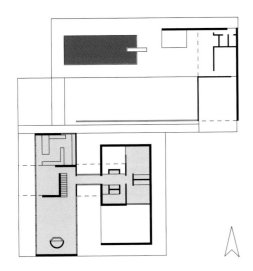

Ground plan

Right:
Sketch of living room

Opposite page, above:
Perspective of entrance

Opposite page, below:
Aerial perspective

1958 ▶ **CSH#20, Bass House**

N. Santa Rosa Avenue, Altadena
Buff, Straub and Hensman

Opposite page:
Terrace
Outdoor chair by Eero Saarinen, manufactured by
Knoll Associates Inc. Outdoor table by Charles and
Ray Eames, manufactured by Herman Miller

Right:
Living Room
Lounge chair (red) by Eero Saarinen, manufactured
by Knoll Associates Inc. Small lounge chairs by
Hans Olsen

Although equally inspired by the goal of applying industrially prefabricated components to residential architecture, the Bass House represents a departure from others in the Case Study program. Constructed of wood rather than steel, and relying heavily on the curving forms of barrel vaults and broad roof overhangs, the house reveals a closer association with the heritage of the Craftsman style and thus reflects its regional setting in Pasadena. The architects were keenly interested in the possibilities of wood construction enabled through the technology of mass production; at the same time, they shared with the clients—a designer and a biochemist—a preference for plasticity and sculptural form. They introduced such features not only in the curving interior ceiling spaces but also in a circular brick fireplace, an ovoid pool, and the dramatic lean of a large pine tree on the site, which was incorporated within an open eave of the house's rear roof overhang.

Kitchen with view to living area

Right:
Site plan

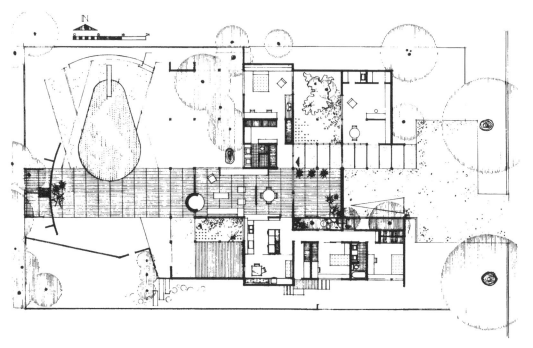

Living room and terrace

Left:
Longitudinal section

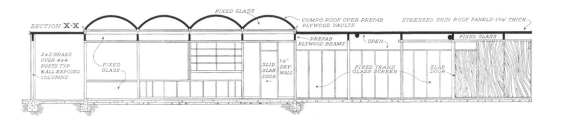

SECTION **X-X**

FIXED GLASS

COMPO ROOF OVER PREFAB PLYWOOD VAULTS

STRESSED SKIN ROOF PANELS-1⅜" THICK

2x3 GRABS OVER 4x4 POSTS TYP @ALL EXPOSED COLUMNS

FIXED GLASS

PREFAB PLYWOOD BEAMS

OPEN

FIXED GLASS

SLID SLAB DOOR

½" DRY-WALL

FIXED TRANS GLASS SCREEN

SLAB DOOR

1958–1960 ▸ CSH#21

Wonderland Park Avenue, West Hollywood
Pierre Koenig

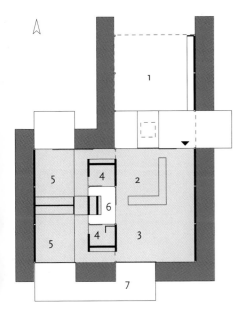

Ground plan
1 Carport, 2 Kitchen, 3 Living room, 4 Bathroom,
5 Bedroom, 6 Patio, 7 Terrace

This compact steel and glass box, designed for a childless couple and situated in a Hollywood Hills canyon, was an experimental exercise for architect Pierre Koenig in on-site assembly as well as in the immaculate detailing of its steel frame. Set within this charcoal-painted framework were walls of glass alternating with steel decking and gypsum, with a ceiling of exposed ribbed steel decking. Minimal to the point of severity, the geometric form of the house was further emphasized by Koenig's avoidance of roof overhangs. Instead, he employed screens over the glass walls to filter sun and heat. Water elements were conceived as integral to the design; reflecting pools surrounding the house were equipped with a system to hydraulically pump water to the roof, where it would fall back again in fountain-like streams to the pools below. An additional innovation was Koenig's provision of a central utility core containing bathrooms and water heater, situated at the house's center and serving to divide the public and private spaces.

Opposite page:
Carport with view to kitchen and office

Right:
Dining room with view to carport
Chairs by Charles and Ray Eames, manufactured by Herman Miller Inc., c. 1951, produced until about 1965. Painted steel wire, vinyl 2-piece seat pad. Table by Charles and Ray Eames, manufactured by Herman Miller Inc., c. 1951, produced until about 1965. Laminated plywood, rubber foam and aluminum base

Opposite page:
Kitchen and living room

Left:
Exterior seen from the north-east

Perspective from patio into bedroom
and living room

1959–1960 ▶ **CSH#22, Stahl House**

Woods Drive, West Hollywood
Pierre Koenig

Opposite page:
Night view of living room

Right:
Exterior and carport seen from the north-west

Among the most radical and reductive designs of the Case Study House program—as well as one of its most iconic images—this house is a simple pavilion situated on a promontory out of view of adjacent houses in the Hollywood Hills. Its L-shaped plan is organized around a swimming pool onto which all the major public rooms and private spaces face; a molded concrete footbridge provides passage over the pool from the carport to the entrance. Using only stock steel components to frame 20-foot wide modules of glass, Pierre Koenig succeeded in maximizing the potential of steel to enclose space in this extraordinarily minimal design. In the interior, the bedrooms occupy one wing of the plan, with dressing room and master bath clustered in the corner of the L adjacent to a utility core and the kitchen. The living wing of the house is entirely open, with steel columns and glass walls interrupted only by the kitchen appliances and cabinets and a freestanding steel fireplace that dominates the living room.

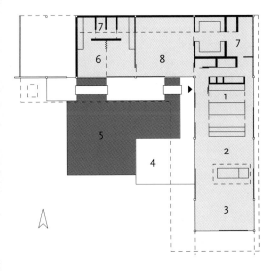

Ground plan
1 Kitchen, 2 Dining room, 3 Living room,
4 Terrace, 5 Pool, 6 Children's room, 7 Bath,
8 Master bedroom

Living room
Ceramic planter probably by Rita Lawrence,
manufactured by Architectural Pottery

Right:
Perspective of living room

Opposite page, above:
**Entrance, patio, and pool with view to kitchen and
living room**

Opposite page, below:
**Perspective of entrance, patio, and pool with view
to kitchen and living room**

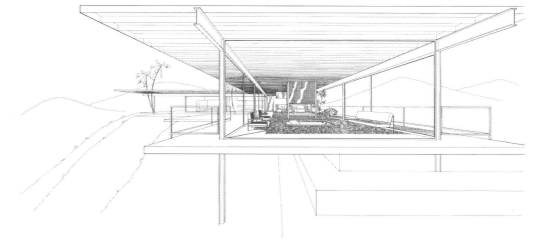

1959–1960 ▶ **CSH#23, "Triad"**

Rue de Anna, La Jolla
Killingsworth, Brady and Smith

Opposite page:
View of House B from House A

Site plan of Houses A, B, and C

This entry into the program ventures toward the idea of multiple housing in that it consists of three adjacent houses designed in relationship to one another. Initially, it was conceived as the pilot project for a much larger tract that was ultimately never built. While the plans of the three houses differed, offering clear variations in the type of living spaces provided, the use of a common vocabulary of materials—wood framing, infill panel walls, concrete slab floors, walnut cabinets throughout, identical appliances and fixtures—established a cohesion among them. However, the exteriors varied significantly from the redwood-paneled exterior of House A, the largest of the three, through the white-painted wood framing of glass walls in House B, to the interplay of translucent glass screening and redwood in House C. Plan innovations in each house were the provision of a family living/dining space distinct from that of the more formal living room, countering the complete elimination of such formal living spaces in the early Case Study designs.

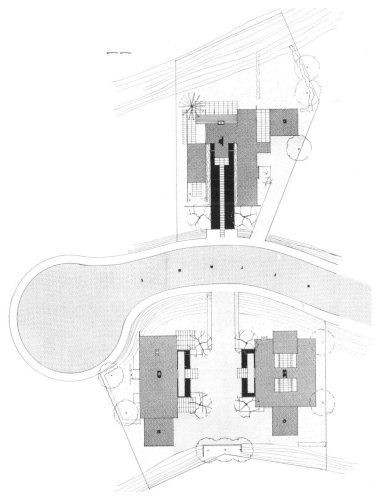

Above:
CSH #23—House A
Entrance

Opposite page:
CSH #23—House B
Patio set by Hendrik van Keppel and Taylor Green,
manufactured by Van Keppel-Green

Below:
CSH #23—House A
Entrance with view to House B

Right:
CSH #23—House A
Ground plan: 1 Entry, 2 Kitchen, 3 Family room,
4 Living room, 5 Bedroom, 6 Bath, 7 Maid, 8 Pool,
9 Garage

Right below:
CSH #23—House B and House C
Ground plan: 1 Entry, 2 Living room, 3 Family room,
4 Kitchen, 5 Bedroom, 6 Bath, 7 Pool,
8 Garage

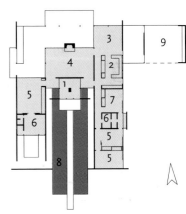

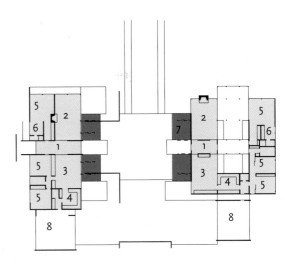

Opposite page:
CSH #23—House C
Living room and terrace

Right:
CSH #23—House C
View of entrance from House B

CSH #23—House C
Patio furniture by Hendrik van Keppel and Taylor
Green, manufactured by Van Keppel-Green

1961 ▶ **CSH#24**

unbuilt
A. Quincy Jones and Frederick E. Emmons

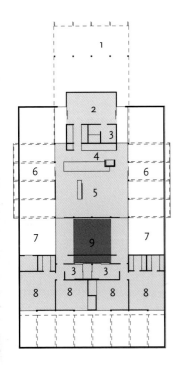

Jones and Emmons' concept for a proposed tract of Eichler Homes contributed a profoundly innovative approach not only to the idea of community planning but also to the design of the individual house. Envisioned as a tract of 260 houses on land near Northridge, the master plan provided space for a park and recreation center for the community by decreasing the size of individual building lots. Five house prototypes would be offered to residents, one of which was designed in some detail as a four bedroom, three bath house offering the utmost in interior flexibility. Jones and Emmons further innovated with the siting of the house prototype, positioning it partially below ground to minimize noise and visual intrusions from adjacent houses as well as attempting to create greater energy efficiency along with a rooftop circulating water system for cooling. Neither their design for the house nor the tract was ultimately realized, owing to prevailing conservative attitudes against providing communal facilities at the expense of individual land ownership.

Ground plan
1 Carport, 2 Multipurpose room, 3 Bath,
4 Kitchen, 5 Living, 6 Shade garden,
7 Sun garden, 8 Bedroom, 9 Pool

**Exterior perspective
showing landscaping**

Opposite page:
**Sectional axonometry of main interior
living spaces**

1962 ▶ CSH#25, Frank House

Rivo Alto Canal, Long Beach
Killingsworth, Brady, Smith and Associates

Opposite page:
**Double-height interior courtyard
and entrance**

Below:
Perspective of rear exterior

Situated on a canal in the Naples section of Long Beach, Case Study House #25 is a double-height structure that presents a closed façade to the exterior but creates its own sense of luxurious space within. Designed for client Edward Frank, whose firm, Frank Brothers, was one of the most important providers of modern furnishings in southern California, the house is approached by means of a pathway of stepping stones over a reflecting pool. Opening the 17-foot-high front door reveals a lath-covered two-story interior courtyard with views into the adjacent living room on the lower level and a bedroom and study above. This relatively compact, yet dramatic, plan conceals additional interior spaces (kitchen, dining room, utility room, additional bedrooms, stair) alongside those that overlook the courtyard. Framed in wood and with smoothly plastered surfaces, the house projects an air of opulence, drama, and relaxed elegance.

Interior courtyard with view to
living room, dining room, and bedroom

Below:
Perspective of exterior from the adjacent canal

Roof terrace
Chairs by Harry Bertoia, manufactured by Knoll
International, c. 1952. Table by Eero Saarinen,
manufactured by Knoll International, c. 1957

Below left:
Exterior seen from the canal

Below right:
Plan of lower level
1 Courtyard, 2 Living, 3 Dining, 4 Kitchen,
5 Service, 6 Bath, 7 Garage, 8 Carport

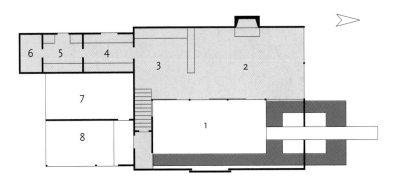

1962–1963 ▶ CSH#26, Harrison House

San Marino Drive, San Rafael
Beverley (David) Thorne

Opposite page:
Rear exterior from hillside below

Right:
Entrance from carport

Below:
Site plan
1 Foyer, 2 Breakfast, 3 Kitchen, 4 Family,
5 Dining, 6 Living, 7 Bedroom, 8 Patio

Located in San Rafael, California, this house was sponsored as a demonstration project by Bethlehem Steel Company and Twentieth Century Homes. Although it was sited on a sloping hillside, architect Thorne configured a design for a four-bedroom, two-bath home on one level without significant excavation. His solution was to place the main spaces of the house below that of the entry/carport, creating a kind of "space platform." This living level was supported by concrete caissons, over which a steel framework on a structural module of 10 feet was positioned. All major rooms of the house, except the kitchen, breakfast room, and foyer, are situated along the rear of the house, faced by sliding glass walls offering access to an open deck and panoramic view. Thorne planned an addition to the house in 1963—an enclosure of the underfloor space to provide an additional 1,400 square feet for guest quarters, maid's room, rumpus room, storage, and a swimming pool.

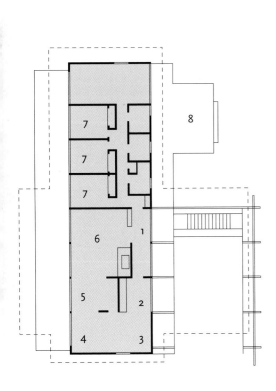

1962 ▶ **CSH#26**

unbuilt
Killingsworth, Brady, Smith and Associates

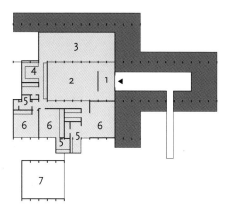

Case Study House #26, an unrealized design by the same architects for a speculative home in San Diego, was based on an experimental prefabricated construction system of concrete and styrene foam. Differing from the custom nature of the Frank House, the goal of this prototype was to drastically reduce the amount of time needed for construction of housing.

1963 ▸ CSH#27

unbuilt
Campbell and Wong

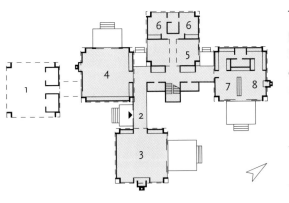

This unrealized house was sponsored by the Richard S. Robbins Company as a prototype for mass production of residences made with precast concrete. Designed for an East Coast site in New Jersey, it consisted of a group of five units connected by passageways, with the goal of allowing each unit a direct relationship to the natural surrounding of the wooded site. This plan situated the living room unit, with its own formal entry, at a slightly greater distance from the rest of the compound, which included modules for the kitchen/dining room/den, master bedroom and study, children's wing with bedrooms and playroom, and carport. The scheme provided the possibility for future expansion, through the provision of additional units or by building a second story onto an existing one. Topped by pyramidal roofs, the precast concrete modules required no interior walls or columns, and their forms contrasted with that of the flat-roofed passageways serving as connectors between them.

Opposite page above:
Ground plan
1 Entry, 2 Garden room, 3 Living room/
Dining room, 4 Kitchen, 5 Bath, 6 Bedroom,
7 Garage

Opposite page below:
Scale model

Elevation looking south-east

Top:
Ground plan
1 Carport, 2 Entry, 3 Living room, 4 Family,
5 Play room, 6 Bedroom, 7 Study, 8 Master
bedroom

1965–1966 ▶ CSH#28

Inverness Road, Thousand Oaks
Buff and Hensman

Opposite page:
Courtyard and pool

Exterior

The last single-family house to be promoted under the aegis of the Case Study House program, this home was designed by architects Buff and Hensman for the Janss Development Company and Pacific Clay Products. Extremely large for a Case Study—almost 5,000 square feet—it utilized facebrick as a major building material, which was also to characterize an entire development of houses in the Thousand Oaks area near Los Angeles. The design is a hybrid, in which the massivity and heaviness of the brick material, which conceals the steel framing structure, is alleviated by extensive areas of glass, the presence of clerestory windows, and multiple open courtyards. In addition, the textured surface of the brick and its deliberate manipulation by the architects add elements of sculptural plasticity to the house's appearance. Symmetrical in plan, it provides an expansive central courtyard, at the center of which is a swimming pool.

Living room with view to dining room
Chairs by Charles and Ray Eames, manufactured
by Herman Miller, c. 1965. Molded fiberglass,
cast polished aluminum

Right:
Dining area
Chairs "DKR-I" by Charles and Ray Eames,
manufactured by Herman Miller, c. 1951. Painted
wire, upholstered seat pad. Wall shelves "CSS"
by George Nelson, manufactured by Herman Miller,
c. 1958. Extruded aluminum, walnut shelves

Interior corridor with view to
courtyard and pool

Left:
Ground plan
1 Carport, 2 Gallery, 3 Living room, 4 Dining
room, 5 Kitchen, 6 Family room, 7 Bedroom,
8 Bath, 9 Swimming pool

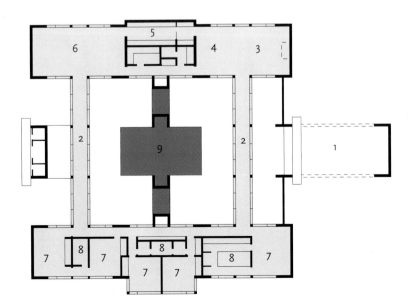

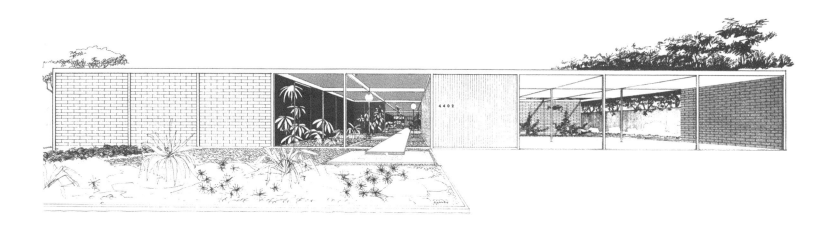

1963 – 1964 ▶ Case Study Apartment #1

28th Street, Phoenix, Arizona
Alfred N. Beadle and Alan A. Dailey

Opposite page, above:
Perspective from the building's entrance

Opposite page, below:
Entrance to an individual unit

Right:
Carport and entrance seen from the north-east

Built in Phoenix, Arizona, this small apartment complex was intended as the first phase of a complex of altogether eighty units, and while this larger effort was not achieved, it stands as the Case Study program's most extensive realized example of multiple housing. The project attempted to rethink the design of the conventional apartment, providing three one-bedroom units of 840 square feet. Each of these compact units contained a living room, kitchen, bath, and study, as well as a private outdoor patio. Communal facilities included carport, storage and laundry, and a central court and walkway bisecting the building's layout around which the three apartments were organized. Materials common to those of the Case Study houses were used in the building's construction—wood framing with alternating walls of plywood and floor-to-ceiling glass, with exterior walls of concrete block.

Ground plan
1 Kitchen, 2 Bath, 3 Bedroom, 4 Study,
5 Living, 6 Carports, 7 Laundry, 8 Storage

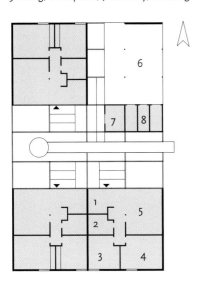

1964 ▶ **Case Study Apartment #2**

unbuilt
Killingsworth, Brady & Associates

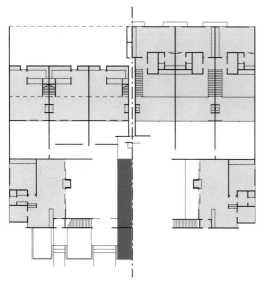

The last of the Case Study projects to take on the problem of multi-family housing, this design for an apartment complex to be situated in Newport Beach envisioned ten units on a lot originally zoned for twelve. In contrast to the first built Case Study Apartments, these two-bedroom units were to be more spacious than the average such dwelling, and as a complex they offered compositional variation. Six of the ten units were designed with two stories and closely resembled the configuration of Case Study House #25, the Frank House, in Long Beach in terms of their access via a tall doorway into a double-height glass-walled interior. The remaining one-story units were equally elegant in their provision of spacious entries and private courtyards. As a further extension of the ideas put forth in the earlier design for house #25, the materials envisioned here were wood framing and plaster, set on an elevated concrete slab and incorporating a reflecting pool.

Above:
Lower level (left) and upper level (right) plans

Right:
Overhead perspective of a unit's living room and terrace

Below:
Perspective from entrance

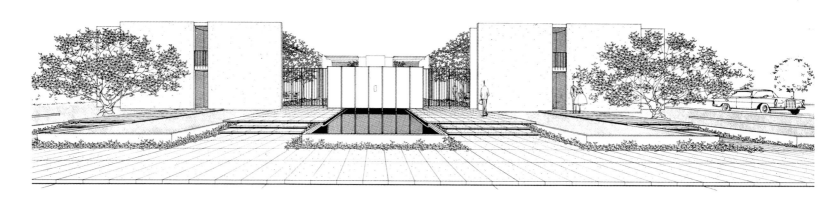

Los Angeles

Bibliography

Credits

▶ *Arts & Architecture* magazine from January 1945 to September 1966 documents the Case Study House program extensively.

▶ Banham, Reyner, Los Angeles: The Architecture of Four Ecologies. New York: Harper and Row, 1971.

▶ Gössel, Peter, Ed. Julius Schulman: Architecture and its Photography. Cologne, New York: Taschen, 1998.

▶ Hines, Thomas S. Richard Neutra and the Search for Modern Architecture: A Biography and History. New York: Oxford University Press, 1982.

▶ Jackson, Neil. California Modern: The Architecture of Craig Ellwood. New York: Princeton Architectural Press, 2002.

▶ Kirkham, Pat. Charles and Ray Eames: Designers of the Twentieth Century. Cambridge, Mass.: MIT Press, 1995.

▶ McCoy, Esther. Case Study Houses 1945–1962. 2nd ed. Los Angeles: Hennessey & Ingalls, Inc., 1977.

▶ McCoy, Esther. Craig Ellwood: Architecture. Santa Monica, Calif.: Hennessey + Ingalls, 1968.

▶ McCoy, Esther, The Second Generation. Salt Lake City, Utah: Gibbs M. Smith, Inc., 1984.

▶ Smith, Elizabeth A. T. et al. Blueprints for Modern Living: History and Legacy of the Case Study Houses. Los Angeles: Museum of Contemporary Art; Cambridge, Mass.: MIT Press, 1989.

▶ Smith, Elizabeth A. T. Case Study Houses: The Complete CSH Program 1945–1966. Cologne, London, New York: Taschen, 2002.

▶ Steele, James/Jenkins, David. Pierre Koenig. London: Phaidon, 1998.

▶ Steele, James, Ed. Buff & Hensman/Donald C. Hensman. New York: University of California Architectural Guild Press, 2004.